Bel the Weather Girl

SPINNING WIND AND WATER

HURRICANES

BELINDA JENSEN

illustrations by Renée Kurilla

series consultant: Lisa Bullard

M Millbrook Press/Minneapolis

To my mom, Jackie, who has always been my biggest cheerleader, and to my dad, Ken, who has always questioned my actions and in doing so spurred me on to be the best I can be. I love you both! —B.J.

For my parents, who kept me company while I was coloring this book! —R.K.

Millbrook Press
A division of Lerner Publishing Group, Inc.
241 First Avenue North
Minneapolis, MN 55401 USA

For reading levels and more information, look up this title at www.lernerbooks.com.

Spiral background: © silm/Shutterstock.com.

Main body text set in ChurchwardSamoa Regular 15/18.
Typeface provided by Chank.

Library of Congress Cataloging-in-Publication Data

Jensen, Belinda, author.
    Spinning wind and water : hurricanes / by Belinda Jensen ; Renée Kurilla, illustrator.
        pages cm — (Bel the Weather Girl)
    Includes bibliographical references and index.
    Audience: 005-007.
    Audience: K to Grade 3.
    ISBN 978-1-4677-7962-3 (lb : alk. paper) — ISBN 978-1-4677-9749-8 (pb : alk. paper) — ISBN 978-1-4677-9750-4 (eb pdf)
    1. Hurricanes—Juvenile literature. 2. Severe storms—Juvenile literature. I. Kurilla, Renée, illustrator. II. Title.
    QC944.2.J46 2016
    551.55'2—dc23   2015015837

Manufactured in the United States of America
1 - CG - 12/31/15

TABLE OF CONTENTS

Chapter One
Hurricane Season

Bel gave her grandfather a hug. "I'm so glad Mom has that meteorology meeting! I love visiting you and Grandma!" she said.

"And I'm glad I got to come along. I love Florida!" said her cousin Dylan.
"Back home, fall means raking leaves. But it's like summer here."

"October is still hurricane season," said Grandpa. "In fact, I've been tracking a tropical storm on my laptop."

"Hurricane!" said Dylan. "I didn't come here to be blown away!"

Hurricanes are huge storms that form over ocean waters. They have spinning winds of at least 74 miles (119 kilometers) per hour. Hurricane season in the United States is June through November.

Grandpa put his hand on Dylan's shoulder. "It isn't a hurricane yet," he said. "Come out to the garage. I'll explain. Weather isn't so scary once you understand it!"

Chapter Two
Spinning Clouds

Grandpa pointed at a map. "The ocean is really warm near the equator. It heats the air above the water. Wind forces the warm air currents together and up. The warm, wet air turns into storm clouds."

"I know what's next!" Bel spun a beach ball. "Earth is always spinning like this ball. That makes the clouds start spinning too!"

Hurricanes are a kind of storm known as tropical cyclones. In other parts of the world, hurricanes are called typhoons, cyclones, or willy-willies.

9

"You're right, Bel the Weather Girl!" said Grandpa. "Then what?"

"Sometimes the clouds get bigger," Bel said. "The spinning winds get faster. The tropical storm turns into a hurricane!"

Dylan looked worried. "I guess we better get out of town, quick!" said Dylan. "Even though it looks way too nice out for a big storm."

The "eye" is a calm area in the center of a hurricane. North of the equator, winds spin counterclockwise around the eye. South of the equator, winds spin clockwise.

Chapter Three

Hurricane Ready

Grandpa tapped the map. "The storm I'm watching is way out here. It's moving slowly. And it looks like it'll miss Florida. It hasn't reached hurricane strength yet. Lots of storms never do."

"Meteorologists are watching it too," said Bel. "Hurricanes take days to grow. We'll have time to get ready if we need to, Dylan."

On average, the United States is hit by about two hurricanes per year. But every hurricane season is different.

13

"I've planned ahead for hurricanes," said Grandpa. "I have storm shutters to put over the windows. I also have supplies for our emergency kit."

Grandpa ruffled Dylan's hair. "Sometimes we do leave town. Hurricane winds can push ocean water up onshore. That's called storm surge. We'd be warned to head inland before that happened."

Hurricanes often produce tornadoes. During a hurricane, it is safest to take shelter in a room without windows.

Chapter Four
Naming the Storm

Bel pulled Dylan back to the map. "Some hurricanes never hit land," she said. "These lines show tracks of past hurricanes. See how many of them died before hitting land?"

FLORIDA

CHRIS '12

Hurricanes are some of the world's biggest storms. They can be 600 miles (966 km) across. Hurricane Inez had wind speeds of 150 miles (240 km) per hour when it hit land.

Dylan looked closer. "Hey! I see a hurricane with Grandma Inez's name. Am I on this map too?"

FRED '09

CAPE VERDE ISLANDS

INEZ '66

FLORENCE '12

BERTHA '14

Grandpa laughed. "Sometimes I call you Hurricane Dylan! But your name isn't on the official hurricane name lists. Each new tropical storm gets the next name on this year's list."

"I have a great idea, Dylan," said Bel. "Why don't you pick a goofy name for this storm? Then it won't seem so scary!"

Tropical storms are given names. There are six lists of names for storms in the Atlantic Ocean. One list is used each year. When a storm is very bad, that name isn't used again. A new name is added to the list.

"Okay, I've got it," said Dylan. "What do you think? Will Tropical Storm Stinky turn into Hurricane Stinky?"

Bel grinned. "We don't know yet. But stay tuned for tomorrow. **Because every day is another weather day!**"

Try It: Make a Hurricane Name List

Hurricane names come from official lists by the World Meteorological Organization. You can check to see if your name is on those lists by visiting the website at www.hurricaneville.com/names.

You probably know lots of names that are not on the official lists. So why not make your own Hurricane Name List just for fun? The World Meteorological Organization uses twenty-one letters of the alphabet. They do not use Q, U, X, Y, and Z. Use your own paper to make a list of letters. Then fill out your list with names of your choosing. You can use names of family members, friends, classmates, pets, or names you make up. The official name lists go back and forth between male names and female names, so make sure your list does too.

A, B, C, D, E, F, G, H, I, J, K, L, M, N, O, P, R, S, T, V, W

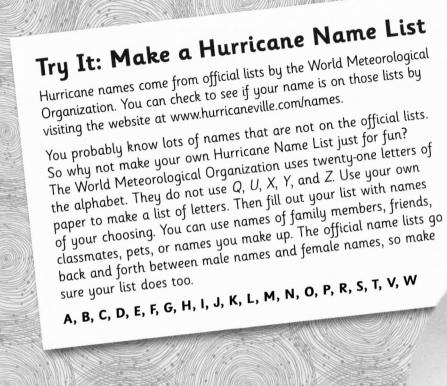

Glossary

clockwise: the direction that the hands of a clock move

counterclockwise: opposite of the direction that the hands of a clock move

current: a body of air moving in a definite direction

cyclones: what hurricanes are called in the South Pacific and Indian Oceans

equator: an imaginary circle around the middle of Earth

hurricane: a huge storm that forms over warm ocean waters and has spinning winds of at least 74 miles (119 km) per hour

inland: away from the coast

meteorologist: a person who is trained to study and predict the weather

meteorology: the science of weather

storm surge: when strong storm winds push water up onshore

tornado: a high-speed, spinning wind that forms during very large storms

tropical: relating to the part of the world near the equator

tropical cyclone: the category of storms that includes hurricanes, cyclones, and typhoons

tropical storm: a storm that forms over warm ocean waters and has winds between 39 miles (63 km) and 73 miles (118 km) per hour

Further Reading

Books

Bodden, Valerie. *Hurricanes*. Mankato, MN: Creative Education, 2012.
Learn more about hurricanes in this book full of facts and photos.

Dean, Janice. *Freddy the Frogcaster and the Huge Hurricane*. Washington, DC: Regnery Kids, 2015.
Read along as Freddy the Frogcaster helps the town of Lilypad prepare for a coming hurricane.

Gibbons, Gail. *Hurricanes!* New York: Holiday House, 2009.
This book is packed full of information about hurricanes and the impact they can have.

Websites

Hurricanes
http://www.ready.gov/kids/know-the-facts/hurricanes
Play a game that will help you learn how to build an emergency kit for your home.

Watch Out . . . Hurricanes Ahead!
http://www.nws.noaa.gov/os/brochures/owlie-hurricane.pdf
Learn more about hurricanes while coloring these pages featuring Owlie from the National Weather Service.

Web Weather for Kids: Hurricanes
https://scied.ucar.edu/webweather/hurricanes
This fact-filled website also includes a story about a child's true experiences in a hurricane.

Index

LERNER

SOURCE

Expand learning beyond the printed book. Download free, complementary educational resources for this book from our website, www.lerneresource.com.